# TOOLS FOR CAREGIVERS

- **F&P LEVEL:** C
- **WORD COUNT:** 37

- **CURRICULUM CONNECTIONS:** nature, leaves, fruit

## Skills to Teach

- **HIGH-FREQUENCY WORDS:** are, I, see, they
- **CONTENT WORDS:** berries, blue, blueberry, buds, closed, green, leaves, open, petals, pink, turn, white
- **PUNCTUATION:** exclamation points, periods
- **WORD STUDY:** compound word (*blueberry*); long /e/, spelled ea (*leaves*); long /e/, spelled ee (*green*, *see*); /oo/, spelled ue (*blue*, *blueberry*)
- **TEXT TYPE:** information report

## Before Reading Activities

- Read the title and give a simple statement of the main idea.
- Have students "walk" through the book and talk about what they see in the pictures.
- Introduce new vocabulary by having students predict the first letter and locate the word in the text.
- Discuss any unfamiliar concepts that are in the text.

## After Reading Activities

Flip back through the book with readers. Ask them what changes about the blueberry plant as it grows. What do they notice about the color of the petals and berries? Can readers name any other plants, fruits, or vegetables that change color as they grow and ripen?

Tadpole Books are published by Jump!, 5357 Penn Avenue South, Minneapolis, MN 55419, www.jumplibrary.com

Copyright ©2023 Jump. International copyright reserved in all countries. No part of this book may be reproduced in any form without written permission from the publisher.

**Editor:** Jenna Gleisner **Designer:** Molly Ballanger

**Photo Credits:** mahirat/Shutterstock, cover; temmuzcan/Shutterstock, 1; P. Qvist/Shutterstock, 2tr, 3; Nahhana/Shutterstock, 2mr, 4–5; Valery Prokhozhy/Dreamstime, 2ml, 2br, 6–7; alfotokunst/Shutterstock, 2bl, 8–9; Oksana Zavadskaya/Shutterstock, 2tl, 10–11; yanjf/iStock, 12–13; Tomasz Pawlus/Shutterstock, 14–15; HildeAnna/Shutterstock, 16.

Library of Congress Cataloging-in-Publication Data
Names: Sterling, Charlie W., author.
Title: Blueberry / by Charlie W. Sterling.
Description: Minneapolis, MN: Jump!, Inc., (2023)
Series: See a plant grow! | Includes index. | Audience: Ages 3–6
Identifiers: LCCN 2021047397 (print) | LCCN 2021047398 (ebook)
ISBN 9781636906935 (hardcover)
ISBN 9781636906942 (paperback)
ISBN 9781636906959 (ebook)
Subjects: LCSH: Blueberries—Life cycles—Juvenile literature.
Classification: LCC SB386.B7 S74 2023 (print) | LCC SB386.B7 (ebook) | DDC 634/.737—dc23
LC record available at https://lccn.loc.gov/2021047397
LC ebook record available at https://lccn.loc.gov/2021047398

# BLUEBERRY

by Charlie W. Sterling

## TABLE OF CONTENTS

tadpole books

# WORDS TO KNOW

**berries**

**buds**

**closed**

**leaves**

**open**

**petals**

# BLUEBERRY

bud

I see buds.

leaf

I see leaves.

petal

I see pink petals.

**They are closed.**

petal

**They turn white.**

They open.

berry ▶

I see berries!

They are green.

berry

I see berries.

**They turn pink.**

berry

I see berries.

# They turn blue!

# LET'S REVIEW!

Blueberries change color as they grow.
What color are the blueberries in this stage?
What color will they turn next?

# INDEX